AF594236

"There is an old proverb that says 'Thoughts disentangle themselves when passing over the lips and through the finger tips.' The 17:18 Series, which encourages us to actually write out the words of Scripture, will be a tremendous tool in putting that proverb into action in our daily lives. I am happy to commend this project."

–Jerry Bridges, a longtime staff member of the Navigators and author of *The Pursuit of Holiness*

"Several years ago I read an article about copying the Scriptures by hand. I tried it with the Pastoral Epistles, writing out all three books with a fountain pen in my journal, and found it a profitable exercise. I am glad to see this series of journals appear, and I hope they are widely used."

–Donald S. Whitney, Associate Professor of Biblical Spirituality, The Southern Baptist Theological Seminary, Louisville

The 17:18 Series

The Book of Ecclesiastes & Song of Solomon

Joel R. Beeke and Rob Wynalda

This book belongs to:

____

Given by: ________________________

Date: ___________________________

Ecclesiastes & Song of Solomon
© 2020 by Full Quiver LLC
www.fullquiver5.com

Published by
Reformation Heritage Books
2965 Leonard St. NE
Grand Rapids, MI 49525
616-977-0889
email: orders@heritagebooks.org
website: www.heritagebooks.org

ISBN 978-1-60178-820-7

Cover Design: Bethany Sanderson and Steve Coy
Journible® Design: Rob Wynalda

Why the 17:18 series?

In Deuteronomy 17, Moses is leaving final instructions concerning the future of Israel. As a prophet of God, Moses foretells of when Israel will place a king over the nation (v. 14). In verses 16 & 17, he lists items that the king could not do as king. In verse 18, he transitions to what he should do as king.

The king is commanded not to simply acquire a copy of the law (the entire book of Deuteronomy) from the "scroll publishing house," but to handwrite his own copy of the law. The purpose of such a copy written by his own hand was so that:

* he would read it
* he would learn to fear the Lord
* he would obey the commands of God
* his heart would not become proud
* he would not turn to the right or the left from following the law (Prov. 4:27)
* also, his sons would serve in the kingdom after him (Deut. 17:19, 20).

Thirty-four hundred years later, educators are "discovering" that students who physically write out their notes by hand have a much greater retention rate than those who simply hear or visually read the information. Apparently, God knew this to be true for the kings of Israel also.

From such understanding came the conception of this series of books.

Have a great time writing and learning the Word of God,

Rob Wynalda
Romans 1:16

The Purpose of the Journible®

Engagement:

The Journible® is a profoundly simple attempt to aid a person's ability to engage the Word of God by slowing down the process of simply reading the text. The book is organized so that the "scribe" can slowly and thoughtfully engage the text while leaving plenty of room to write comments and questions about the text (Deuteronomy 17:18; Psalm 119; 2 Timothy 3:16, 17).

Legacy:

Journibles® provide a legacy to pass on from one generation to the next. The Journible® creates an opportunity for one generation to communicate in writing to the next generation their insights and personal applications of the text (Deuteronomy 6).

How to use this book

This book is organized so that the scribe (you) will handwrite your very own copy of Ecclesiastes & Song of Solomon. You will be writing the text of the Bible only on the right-hand page of the book. This should make for easier writing and also allows ample space on the left page of your open text to write your own notes and comments. From time to time a question or word will be lightly printed on the left page; these questions are to aid in further study, but should not interfere with your own notes and comments. This means that you are encouraged not only to write your own "copy" of the Bible, but also to write your own notes concerning the text.

Yes, we are setting aside our mass-produced Gutenberg Bibles and attempting to get back to the simple handwritten copy of the text.

Notes

(1) What parallels can you find between the Preacher and Solomon as he is described in 1 Kings 4?

(2) What does "all is vanity" reveal about the theme of Ecclesiastes?

(3) How would you answer this question in light of this present life and in light of eternity?

(4–7) How does God's redemptive plan break the cycle of endless frustration?

(8) Why is it vain to live to satisfy your eyes?

2

3

4

5

6

7

8

Notes

(9–10) How does the monotony of life beckon our hearts to seek transcendent purpose?

(12) The Preacher was more privileged than any man on earth, yet he was also more vexed. How do these two facts correspond, and what do they reveal about this world?

(13–14) If seeking wisdom is so noble, why does it make the Preacher feel so frustrated (see Eccl. 8:16–17)?

9

10

11

12

13

14

15

Notes

(18) How do wisdom and knowledge bring grief?

16

17

18

Notes

(1–2) Why is the pursuit of earthly pleasure futile?

(3) What is folly, and how did the Preacher acquaint himself with it without forsaking wisdom?

(4–8) What does the activity of the Preacher reveal about the heart of man?

2

3

4

5

6

7

Notes

(10) What is the danger of giving your heart all that it desires?

(11) What does the Preacher mean that there was "no profit" from all his labor?

(13–16) What do the wise and foolish have in common, and why is that troubling?

8

9

10

11

12

13

Notes

(18–19) Why would the Preacher conclude that he hated the fruit of his work?

14

15

16

17

18

Notes

(23) How does the Preacher's "burdensome work" relate to the curse of Genesis 3:17–19?

(24) What makes a man's labor enjoyable?

19

20

21

22

23

24

Notes

25

26

Notes

(1) Ponder how God's providence in appointing seasons and times applies to the full gamut of life.

(2–8) What is the point of these contrasts, and how is God involved?

(9) How would you answer this question?

Ecclesiastes 3:1-9

1

2

3

4

5

6

7

8

9

Notes

(11) What is the tension between having eternity in man's heart and not finding out God's work?

(12–13) Why is the Preacher not advocating to "eat, drink and be merry" (see Luke 12:19)?

(14) What is so good about what God does?

(16–17) Explain justice and why it is important to our lives.

10

11

12

13

14

15

16

Notes

(18–20) How are the sons of men like beasts?

(21–22) How does God's Word solve the Preacher's philosophical dilemma?

17

18

19

20

21

22

Notes

(1) Contrast this with Revelation 21:4. Why is the Preacher's perspective limited? What can you learn from it?

(6) Why is contentment better than the pursuit of materialistic values (see Prov. 15:16)?

Ecclesiastes 4:1-7

1

2

3

4

5

6

7

Notes

(8) How would you personally answer this question?

(9–12) Why does the Preacher appreciate companionship? How do you pursue meaningful friendships in your life?

(13) What is it that makes a person obviously wise or foolish?

8

9

10

11

12

13

Notes

14

15

16

Notes

(1) How does one walk prudently when going to the house of God? What is "the sacrifice of fools"?

(4) What does God's concern over a vow teach us about Him?

(6–7) How would you know if you feared God?

1

2

3

4

5

6

Notes

(8–9) Since sinners govern in society, why is orderly rule better than anarchy?

(10–12) How do these verses expose the futility of the materialistic worldview?

7

8

9

10

11

12

13

Notes

(16) How do you avoid chasing or laboring for the wind in your life (see also 1 Cor. 9:24–27)?

(18–20) What is a gift from God? How can we enjoy it without abusing it?

14

15

16

17

18

19

Notes

20

Notes

(2) Why are God's temporal gifts inferior to His eternal gifts?

(6) Why is it wise to think deeply about the brevity of life (see Ps. 90:12)?

Ecclesiastes 6:1-7

1

2

3

4

5

6

7

Notes

(9) Why is contentment with your life better than coveting someone else's life?

(10) Why is it unwise to contend with God by being discontented with your circumstances?

(12) Since life is but a "shadow," how should we then live?

8

9

10

11

12

Notes

(2) Why does the Preacher think the house of mourning is better than feasting?

(4) Why is the wise found in the house of mourning?

(5) What is the song of fools, and how is it contrasted with the wise?

(7) Why is a bribe so evil?

(8) How do the first and second halves of this verse relate? Why is patience wise? How does pride engender impatience?

Ecclesiastes 7:1-8

1

2

3

4

5

6

7

8

Notes

(9) Do you ever get angry? How can you mortify sinful anger?

(11–12) What makes wisdom of greater value than earthly treasures?

(13–14) What is the Preacher revealing to us about God? Why is despair not the right response to life's unjust, or "crooked," things?

9

10

11

12

13

14

15

Notes

(16–18) What are the two excesses of life, and why are they dangerous?

(20) What does the Preacher recognize about man? Why is this important?

16

17

18

19

20

21

22

23

Notes

(26) What is more bitter than death? Why?

24

25

26

27

28

29

Notes

(4) How does the authority of a king's word point you to esteem the authority of God's Word?

(5) Explain what a wise man discerns and why it matters.

Ecclesiastes 8:1-7

1

2

3

4

5

6

7

Notes

(8) If we are powerless to stop death, why should we think about it?

(11) What leads to man's deception? Apply this to your life.

(12–13) How does reckoning with eternal judgment inform our lives now?

Ecclesiastes 8:8-12

8

9

10

11

12

Notes

(15–17) Explain how the Preacher's pessimism points to ultimate meaning in life.

13

14

15

16

17

Notes

(1) Why is it wise for us to contemplate God's exhaustive sovereignty over our lives?

(2–3) Why should you not determine God's disposition toward you based on the circumstances of life?

(4–6) What is the point concerning the dog and the lion?

Ecclesiastes 9:1-5

1

2

3

4

5

Notes

(10) How should the brevity of life inform our work ethic?

6

7

8

9

10

11

Notes

(12) How does God's Word encourage us when we are ensnared by life's tragedies?

(16) Why is it ironic that wisdom is not highly valued in the world?

(18) Apply this verse to your life.

12

13

14

15

16

17

18

Notes

(1) How easily is one's good testimony for wisdom destroyed?

(3) How can we easily identify a fool (read Prov. 7)?

(5–7) How does the irony of life's incongruities tie into the theme of "vanity"?

Ecclesiastes 10:1-8

1

2

3

4

5

6

7

8

Notes

(10) How does this metaphor apply to all the activities of life? What about spiritual disciplines? Ordinary vocational duties? How can you "sharpen your axes"?

(11) How does this verse apply to wisdom?

(12–15) What does a fool do?

(16) What is wrong with a morning feast? How would you apply this today?

9

10

11

12

13

14

15

16

Notes

(20) Why is there never a time when we should not watch our words?

17

18

19

20

Notes

(1) What does it mean to cast your bread upon the waters?

(4) How would a proper view of God remedy the problems spoken of in this verse?

(5) Read Psalm 139. What is the Preacher recognizing?

(6) What is the principle the Preacher is getting at, and how can we apply it today?

Ecclesiastes 11:1-7

1

2

3

4

5

6

7

Notes

(9–10) What advice is the Preacher giving, and how is his advice similar to the advice given in Proverbs?

8

9

10

Notes

(1) What does it mean to remember your Creator, and what does this warning teach about God?

(2–8) What is the Preacher describing, and what does he encourage as a proper response?

1

2

3

4

5

Notes

(10) How are these words upright, acceptable, and words of truth?

(11) Who do you think the "one shepherd" is (see Ps. 23:1; Ezek. 34:23; John 10:16)?

(12) How does this verse suggest we should treasure the choice words of inspired wisdom in the Bible?

6

7

8

9

10

11

12

Notes

(13–14) What is the sum and conclusion of the whole book of Ecclesiastes? After all is written, why isn't the Preacher in despair?

13

14

Notes

(1) What is meant by "the song of songs"?
Why the repetition of "song"?
(2) Why should we yearn for manifestations of Christ's love more than the choicest earthly delights?

(4) How does the Shulamite's intimacy of covenantal union and communion with the king point to the church's consummate union with Christ (see Hosea 1–3; Eph. 5:25–27)?

1

2

3

4

5

6

7

Notes

(8–10) What kind of love does he have for the Shulamite? How does this reflect God's love for His people (see Zeph. 3:17)?

(13) How is the beloved like a bundle of myrrh?

(15–16) How do they express their mutual love, and how does this apply to Christ and His church?

8

9

10

11

12

13

14

15

16

17

Notes

(1) What is meant by the rose of Sharon?
Who is this pointing to?
(2) Who is speaking, and how does what he says complement the previous verse?

(3) Has Christ's fruit aroused the affections of your heart today or in the past week or month? How has your life shown this?

(4) What is the purpose of a banner, and why was it special to her?

(7) How does the refrain in the last part of this verse relate to the message of the book?

1

2

3

4

5

6

7

8

Notes

(10–13) Why is the Beloved describing the spring season?

9

10

11

12

13

14

15

Notes

(16) Why is the mutual possession of each other appropriate? How does Christ lay hold on us, and we on Him?

16

17

Notes

(1–2) What line is repeated in these verses? Why?

(3) Who are the watchmen, and what does the Shulamite want to know from them?

(4) How does her grip on her beloved inform us about how we should embrace Christ?

(5) How can you take this counsel to heart and teach others likewise?

(6–10) Based on this procession, how is Christ similar to Solomon?

1

2

3

4

5

6

7

Notes

(11) What is significant about the daughters of Zion beholding the majesty of Solomon?

8

9

10

11

Notes

(1–6) Why is passionate love so particular in the praises of its object?

(7) Is it possible that the Shulamite was really perfect in appearance? What does this reveal about the Beloved's love toward her?

Song of Solomon 4:1-7

1

2

3

4

5

6

7

Notes

(8) What is the Beloved requesting? Why?

(9–11) How do you think the Beloved's bride feels?
How should the church feel about Christ's love toward her?

8

9

10

11

12

13

14

Notes

(15) How important was "living" water in the life of Israel, and how did Jesus speak of it?

(16) Why is it significant that love is portrayed as idealistic delight in a paradise garden (see Gen. 2:24–25)?

15

16

Notes

(2) What does it mean that she was sleeping yet her heart was awake?

(3–6) Do the church's sloth and excuses result in loss of communion with Christ?

Song of Solomon 5:1-6

1

2

3

4

5

6

Notes

(7) Why is she with the watchmen, and why would they strike her?

(9) What are the daughters of Jerusalem asking? What makes Christ unique?

(10–16) She finds nothing but majesty, delight, riches, and pleasure in her beloved. Meditate on this particularly in relation to the beauties of Christ.

7

8

9

10

11

12

13

Notes

14

15

16

Notes

(3) What is significant about saying "I am my beloved's, and my beloved is mine"? How does such assurance bring joy and delight?

(4) Explain the three ways in which he praises her (see also v.10).

(5) What does this poetic language intend to communicate about the Beloved's affection for the bride?

(8–9) How does he view the Shulamite compared to all others?

Song of Solomon 6:1-8

1

2

3

4

5

6

7

8

Notes

9

10

11

12

13

Notes

(1) Why does he love the way the Shulamite walks? Does your walk please the Lord?

(3–7) How many times does he mention her breasts, and what does this communicate not only at the marital level but spiritually?

Song of Solomon 7:1-7

1

2

3

4

5

6

7

Notes

(10) What does this have in common with Psalm 45:11, and how does the larger context of that Psalm inform our reading of the Song of Songs?

(11) Why does the Shulamite call out for her beloved to "come"? Why should the church call out to Christ?

(13) What do the mandrakes symbolize (see Gen. 30:14)? How does this fit the message of this book?

8

9

10

11

12

13

Notes

(1) Why did she wish he were like a brother?

(2) What does she mean by the house of her mother?

(6–7) What makes the love of God invincible and enduring? Read 1 Corinthians 13. How does Christ perfectly incarnate the reality of these verses?

1

2

3

4

5

6

(8) Who do you think the little sister is? What is the application today?

(9) Why would they enclose her?

(10) How does Christ's love alone give His bride ultimate "peace" (Heb. shalom)?

7

8

9

10

11

12

Notes

(14) Why does the book end with the Shulamite calling out for her beloved to come quickly (see Rev. 22:20)?

13

14

Notes

Notes

Notes

Notes

Notes